THE SEARCH FOR KING

A FABLE

THOMAS SMITH

Printed in the United States of America
Hardcover ISBN: 978-1-959096-35-1
Paperback ISBN: 978-1-959096-36-8
eBook ISBN: 978-1-959096-37-5

Library of Congress Control Number: 2023934562

**Canoe Tree
Press**

4697 Main Street
Manchester Center, VT 05255

Canoe Tree Press is a division of DartFrog Books

This is dedicated to the family I never expected.
To my lovely and loving wife.
To the owners of the 10 other stocking hung
by the chimney with care.

My thanks to Alex Hopping for his ornithological expertise and his careful review of every bird photo and every bird word in the book. My special thanks to Christine Havens and Robert George for their ongoing encouragement, review, critique and support.

The Search for King is not based on any citable publications. The information about birds and wording in footnotes is taken from numberous websites. None are referenced specifically, as all of the information is common knowledge among bird enthusiests and is basically the same on the various websites. These include:

All About Birds	Bird Feeder Hub
(Cornell Ornithology Lab)	Bird Watching HQ
Animal Corner	DiscoverWildlife
Animal Spot	Fun Facts 4 Kids
Audubon Society	Wikipedia
Bird Advisors	Wild Birds Unlimited

CONTENTS

FOREWORD

This book is about birds. The photos of birds are great. I can say this without conceit since none of them are mine. The poetry is about birds. I think that it is interesting and that it is different. I say this with all conceit since all of the poetry is mine. I hope you find the photos and poetry contribute to your enjoyment of birds. This tells a story about diversity, acceptance, and personal values. It is a story about pride and ego. It has a happy ending. Who becomes king is recognition of the moral of the story.

In the story, in order to be elected king, it is a requirement for a bird to have black feathers. The first birds to present this are blackbirds, of course. I chose the color black because it is a color of feathers that most birds have. It fits into the purpose of the story. I could not find another color—not yellow or blue or any other possibility—that most birds share. It also made it easy to talk about thinking "in black and white." "Everything is black and white" is about extremes and polarizations.* Life often is complex and full of all the shades of gray.

---

* https://healthline.com/health/mental-health/black-and-white-thinking/

AND THE STORY BEGINS

VII

Genesis 1

[20]And God said, "...let birds fly above the earth across the vault of the sky." [21]So God created...every winged bird according to its kind. And God saw that it was good. [22]God blessed them and said, "Be fruitful and increase in number...and let birds increase on the earth."

The birds needed to elect a king.

The birds flocked to the Meeting Tree.
Blackbirds made a quick decree:
Black feathers will be compulsory
For the bird that king will be.
Blackbirds' intent was not hard to see,
To make one of them the nominee.

Animals are classified by Class > Order > Family > Genus > Species. Birds are categorized as the biologic Class named Aves, so king of Class would be Head of Birds.

THE COMMON BLACKBIRD

Blackbird went first and chose his words
To try to dazzle the other birds,
Blackbird's pie a story told,
Came from a pirate very bold;
Actually, was Blackbeard's code,
Blackbirds were crewmen who were stowed.
"My mother told me to keep sharp eyes,
Cats and cars bring my demise.
I am the blackest bird around,
I'm the one who should be crowned,
I'm the bird you can't surpass,
You know I should be king of Class.

Red-winged Blackbirds roost in flocks in all months of the year. Winter flocks can be congregations of several million birds, including other blackbird species and starlings.

THE RED-WINGED BLACKBIRD

Suddenly a bird flew in,
Was black to Blackbird's true chagrin.
He was just as black but all admired
What Red–winged Blackbird had acquired.
Red epaulets on wings each side
He wore with something more than pride.
All in all, it must be said,
His epaulets were very red.
"I say it with great modesty,
I have the mien of royalty,
I deserve your loyalty,
I know it's king I'll someday be."

This native North American bird reminded the earliest European settlers of the scarlet-colored robes and caps of Catholic cardinals.

The Northern Cardinal is the official state bird of seven states: Illinois, Indiana, Kentucky, North Carolina, Ohio, Virginia, and West Virginia.

THE NORTH AMERICAN CARDINAL

A Cardinal landed all astir;
Someone had wrong way rubbed his fur.
"You have a little bit of red
Distinctive only in your head.
How can you be so silly proud,
You think you stand out in a crowd?
I'm seeing red, just look at me
And you'll see red you'll never see
When looking in a blackbird tree.
For seven states the honoree.
I was destined to be king
The moment I began to sing.

One naming option for a group of Yellow-headed Blackbirds is "cloud." Some other collective choices are cluster, grind, flock and merle.

THE YELLOW-HEADED BLACKBIRD

This bird came when calls he heard
(Talking when you are a bird).
He didn't know if the topic was cheerful
Until he came and got an earful.
"I'm a Blackbird, yellow–head,
Never hear a cross word said
Between the birds within my cloud.
But since your talk is very loud
And I have now heard everything,
I know that I will be your king.
My yellow feathers do adorn
Like a crown already worn.

Cowbirds are named for their habit of following cattle in order to prey upon insects stirred up from fields by the cows. They lay their eggs in the nests of other bird species, who then raise the young cowbirds.

A Brown-Headed Cowbird's speckled egg in a Bluebird's nest.

The Brown-headed Cowbird

The Cowbird joined the growing crowd.
He cleared his throat, then said out loud,
"We leave our eggs; you hatch our chicks.
Afterwards they intermix
And you do every bit of rearing.
We thank you all for volunteering.
In return I will agree
To be your king, your royalty.
Certainly, I feel respected,
Qualified to be elected.
I know it is what is expected.
I will be the one selected."

Common Grackles eat almost anything they get. They attack farmlands and destroy large amounts of crops. In urban settings, and they are a threat to car paint.

THE GRACKLE

Another came to make his plea,
A candidate for king was he.
The Grackle said that he was best,
His lovely sheen outshone the rest.
His head an iridescent blue,
With bronzy body that he knew
Made him the finest bird that day.
No doubt the proudest on display,
Not black from crown to toe was he,
what kind of bird king could he be?
"Quiet your chirping; I'll enthrall.
"I am the best dressed of you all."

Folklore says that all European Starlings in North America are descended from 160 birds released in Central Park in 1890–1891 by the American Acclimatization Society. In fact, numerous Starlings had been released by the AA.

Murmuration of Starlings

THE EUROPEAN STARLING

A bird flew down to raise a wing.
"Forgive me, but I'd say a thing."
He was polite, this handsome Starling.
All the birds thought he was darling.
His speed took him both wide and far,
Flying he looked like a star.
He sang the songs of twenty others.
Story is all Starlings are brothers.
"I'm a Blackbird as you can see,
With stellar spots all over me;
So now it is of me I sing,
I am next to be your king."

Bluebirds and other blue birds do not have blue color in their feathers. There are cells in their wings that absorb all colors except blue. Only blue light is reflected off their feathers, resulting in their blue appearance to our eyes.

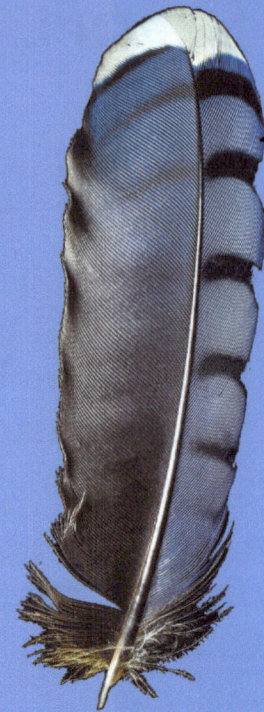

Loss of reflected blue color

THE BLUEBIRD

Bluebird thinks he leads the pack:
Vivid blue seen head and back.
His wings each had a little black,
His place in the race for king intact.
"I guess you know that I'm not blue,
Reflected light has fooled you, too.
I see an insect from up high,
I 'drop hunt' down to eat the guy,
When I'm alone I sing like crazy,
Three hundred songs an hour is lazy.
I'm next to wear the Bird–land crown,
I'm going to win the race wings down.

Originally, a jay was a talkative, impertinent, chatterbox person who tended to dominate conversations. Blue Jays were so named because they tend to be loud, lively, and very vocal.

Green Jay

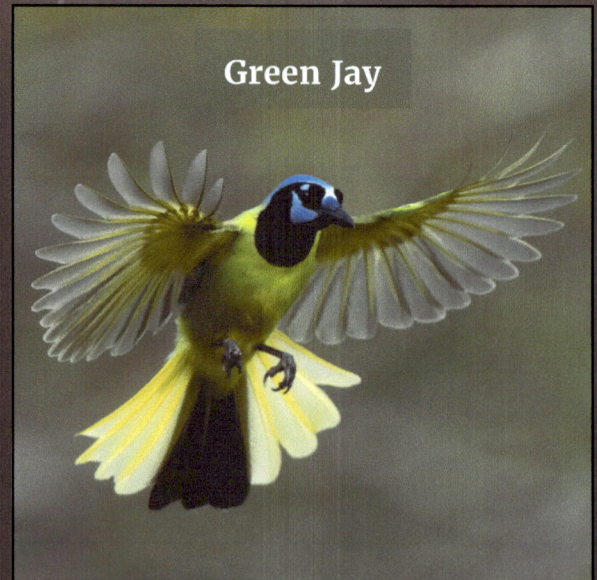

THE BLUE JAY

Blue Jay had some notes to offer;
It was clear he was the author.
Started to address the crowd,
"Other birds say Jays are loud,
Impertinent, ongoing chatter.
Some people also, for that matter.
I will admit I'm colorful,
I'm really smart. I'm wonderful!
I trust that none will ever say
That I am just a popinjay.
My gorgeous blues and black and white,
This Blue Jay should be king outright."

Crows are considered the most intelligent bird. A crow is supposedly as smart as a 7-year-old human child.
A group of crows is called a murder.

THE CROW

Then who came cawwww–ling but the Crow,
"I was afraid to miss the show.
It's entertaining, but I alone
Will be perching on the throne.
You want a black bird as your king?
Well, I'm the biggest blackest thing.
I'm sure you've heard on what I'll dine.
Garbage is, of course, quite fine.
Seeds and insects, all debris,
Not many chicks or birds, you see.
I swear that you are in no danger,
It's not like your king's a stranger."

21

End lines based on "The Raven,"
a poem by Edgar Allen Poe,
published January 29, 1845.
A group of ravens is called an
unkindness because of their
association with bad luck, black
magic, and death.

THE RAVEN

A Raven flew to join the fray,
All wondering what he might say.
Quite a large bird to compare
To every other bird now there.
Blackest of the family,
Aura of authority,
Intelligent and dignified,
Predator exemplified.
His credentials, this he swore,
"Merely this and nothing more.
Make me king, we'll have rapport."

Quoth the Raven, "Evermore."

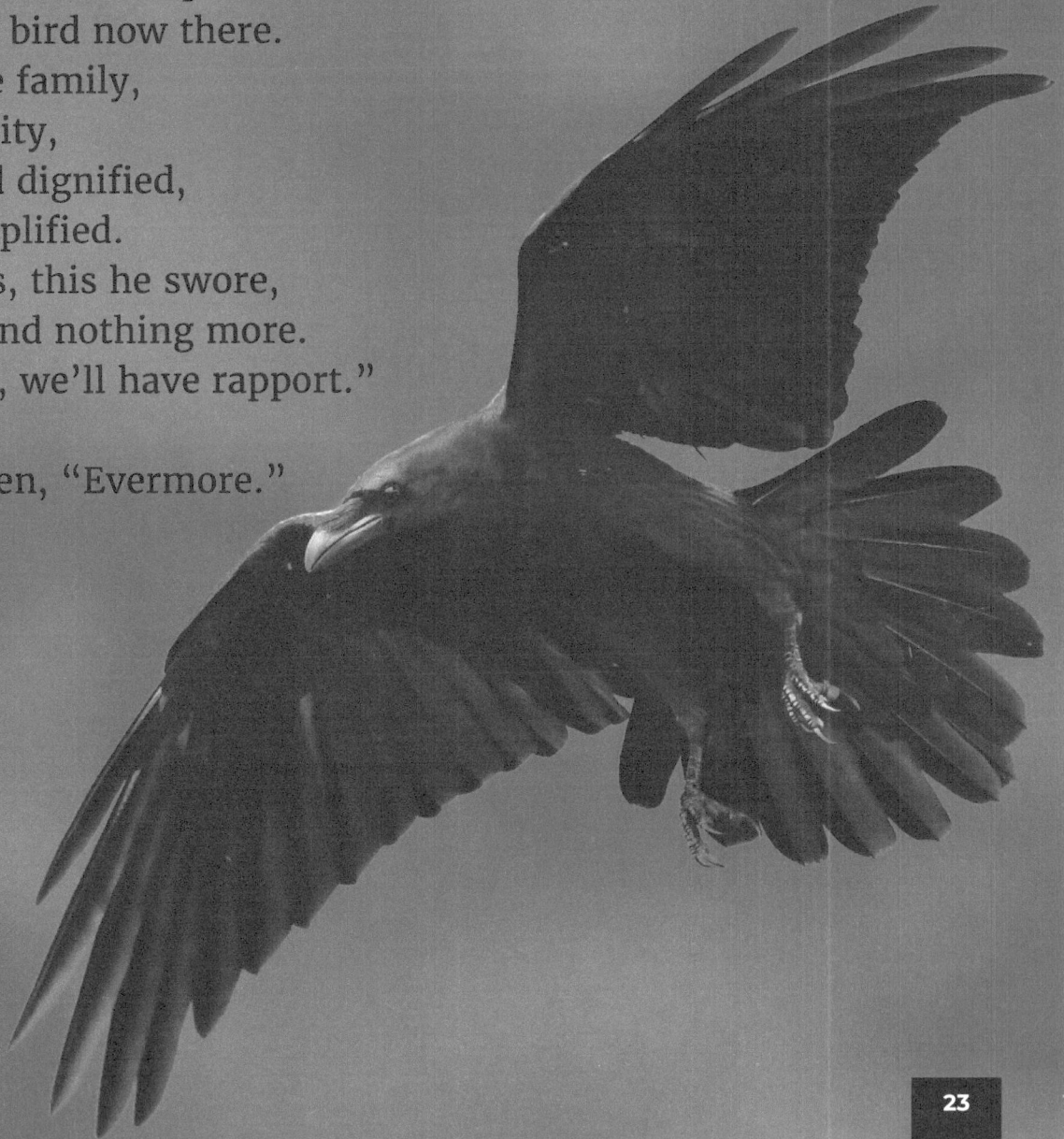

A Northern Mockingbird may have a repertoire of over 200 different songs, and it continues to add new songs throughout its life.

THE NORTHERN MOCKINGBIRD

Mockingbird began to sing,
He sang the sounds of everything:
His own, two hundred songs he quotes,
And any other sounds he notes,
Car alarms and cell phone rings,
He imitates so many things.
"Black tail feathers, black each wing
Qualify me to be your king.
I've been called the 'King of Song',
I've been royalty all long.
I can sing without repeat
For several hours, quite a feat!
I am so clever when I sing,
And that itself should make me king."

The Wren earned the name "king of the birds" in folklore. It once flew higher than an eagle, by clinging to its back and only flying off when the larger bird tired.

Marsh Wren

Pacific Wren

Carolina Wren

THE WREN

And then was when they heard the Wren
With voice that could be fifteen men
That came from such a tiny frame;
Perhaps this was his claim to fame.
Named "King of Birds" in English lore,
There seemed no need to look for more.
"But no," he cried out, "more to me!
More splendid feathers you'll not see.
Tiny markings black on brown,
A brownish reddish wins the crown.
For voice and color I'm the best,
These take me above the rest."

House Wren

American Goldfinches can weave their nests so tightly that it will temporarily hold water. To keep their nests secure in the trees the birds use spider webs. The webbing is used to attach the nest to twigs and even small branches.

THE AMERICAN GOLDFINCH

Another county heard from then,
The Goldfinch was just checking in.
"Brilliant yellow and shiny black,
My color combo is crackerjack.
This bird is a vegetarian.
(Oops, I think I ate a bug again.)
The finest nest to say it right,
It holds water, it's so tight.
Forgive if I might seem too bold,
But I see myself with crown of gold.
I am a harbinger of spring
And also of my being king."

The redder the head, the more virile the male appears to females. To produce their stunning red heads, Western Tanagers need to eat insects that have ingested a rare pigment found in conifer buds.

Western Tanager

Scarlet Tanager

Hepatic Tanager

Summer Tanager

THE WESTERN TANAGER

The Western Tanager chimed in,
"I don't know where I should begin.
"I present as candidate
Myself, because I am so great.
Girls see red and know we're studs
By eating bugs in conifer buds.
I heard the boast that colored wing
Is the most important thing for king,
Then king I am, not any others,
I have the most and brightest colors.
By the way, is it what you want?
A multicolored commandant?
Fantastic, I'm the one to win,
My life's calling should begin."

Painted Buntings are like rainbows in flight. This is probably why they're nicknamed nonpareil or "unparalleled." Males are extremely territorial and will defend their habitat.

THE PAINTED BUNTING

"Birdy, not to break your bubble,
But now you start to ask for trouble.
I've been told I've an angry streak.
Birdland life is not for the meek.
You are simply arrogant;
You are such an embarrassment.
I say this since I am unbiased,
You aren't the brightest in the slightest.
Blue, green, red, brown, black, then yellow,
Plus orange make me quite the fellow.
'Nonpareil' is what they say,
I can brighten any day.
The choice is clear, no further hunting,
Yes, the next king will be this Bunting."

Nuthatches are the only species that can grip tree bark and can walk up and down around tree trunks. They hang upside down on the undersides of tree limbs while foraging for insects and seeds. They're sometimes referred to as "upside-down birds."

White-Breasted Nuthatch

Red-Breasted Nuthatch

Brown-Headed Nuthatch

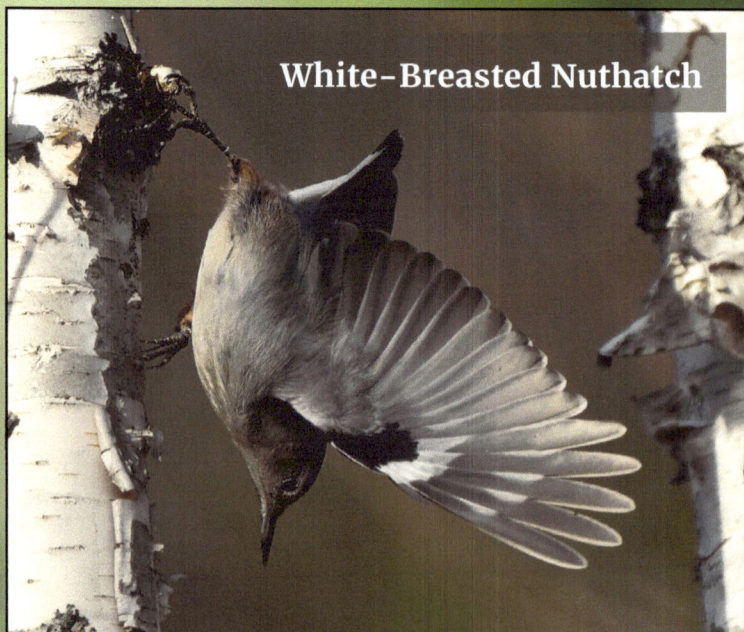
White-Breasted Nuthatch

THE NUTHATCH

This feisty bird has quite a story,
Defending home and territory.
Super power for him could be
Walking upside down a tree.
Nuthatch's name came from his trademark:
He'd put a nut between the tree bark
And use his beak to whack away.
His back is blends of blue and gray,
Black and white were on his head.
"I've got the black," the tough bird said.
"So sign me up, I'll win the vote,
No need to sing another note."

Red–Breasted Nuthatch

The Swallow is called the "bird of freedom" because it cannot endure captivity and will only mate in the wild.

The Barn Swallow

Came the Swallow inward gliding,
Widely known for agile flying.
Eats and drinks while in the air,
Tail and wings both help him there.
Recognized by sailors of yore,
Tattoos that the sailors wore
Marked their number of miles at sea.
Good luck for safe return they'd be.
He told them, "Black is on my face,
That gives me entrance to the race.
This Swallow clearly has the class
To make the Bird-king spot at last!"

Typical Swallow Tattoo

John Ward, often known as Jack, also nicknamed Sparrow, was an actual privateer then pirate in the 16th Century. He was the inspiration for the character in the *Pirates of the Caribbean* film.

Song Sparrow

Eurasian Tree Sparrow

White-crowned Sparrow

House Sparrow

THE HOUSE SPARROW

"I am a Sparrow; call me Jack.
I've never been to sea 'cause I couldn't get back.
I am a little chirpy bird,
No matter what it is you've heard.
Gray and white, and bib of black,
Rufous neck, stripes down my back.
'Notorious' means fame and flair?
I can catch a moth midair.
'Invasive' is just jealousy,
I love humans; they love me.
'Aggressive', well, you've got me there.
Elect me king or you beware!"

Baltimore Orioles sport the same orange-and-black colors as the heraldic crest of England's Baltimore family.

A baseball card is a trading card that often features one or more baseball players. In the 1950s they came with a stick of gum.

THE BALTIMORE ORIOLE

The Oriole said, "Stop right there!
You others must the king forswear.
I am the one to wear the crown,
I make the cut for king wings down.
I wear black on head and back,
Gives me entrance to the pack,
Then watch my brilliant plumage blaze,
With an orange that will amaze.
I sing a rich and whistling song;
When I feel spring, it won't be long.
I have the cards to win this game
And I'll be king to wild acclaim."

Since they can run at speeds over 20 miles per hour and most of their prey is on the ground, roadrunners don't have much of a reason to fly.

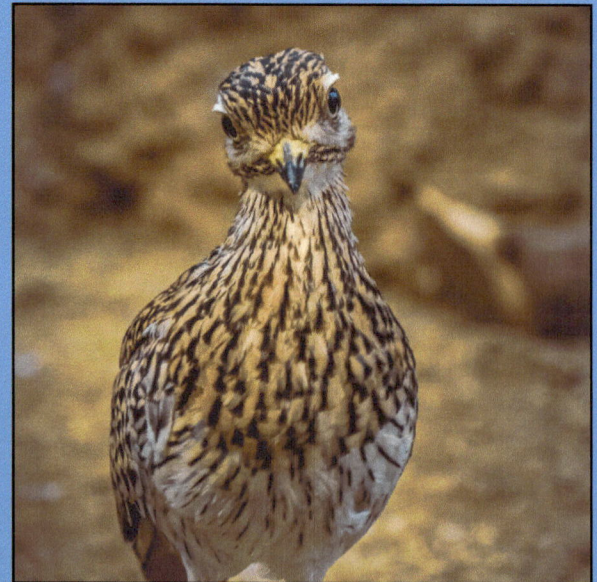

THE ROADRUNNER

"A roadrunner is hard to spot,
Here I am and then I'm not.
When watching me you must concede
A cuckoo with fantastic speed.
I'm long and long and longer still,
My legs and tail and neck and bill.
I don't like to fly, but watch me go.
I mostly can outrun my foe.
I don't beep, in fact, I coo,
I'll also bark and growl at you.
A powerful spirit, I can arrange
Good luck and also help with change.
Blackish streaking back and wing;
My crown is black, I'm surely King."

The name titmouse is recorded from the 14th century, composed of the Old English name for the bird, 'mase', and 'tit', denoting something small.

Bridled Titmouse

Tufted Titmouse

Black-crested Titmouse

Black-crested Titmouse

THE TUFTED TITMOUSE

"I have a funny moniker,
Let me explain to the chronicler.
Titmouse is from two ancient words,
One for small; the other, birds.
My manners are beyond sublime,
I only take one seed each time.
I like one place for every season.
Migrate South? I see no reason.
I make a stash of sunflowers seeds
Which through the winter meet my needs.
Tuft is black on Texas birds.
I will be king, you mark my words."

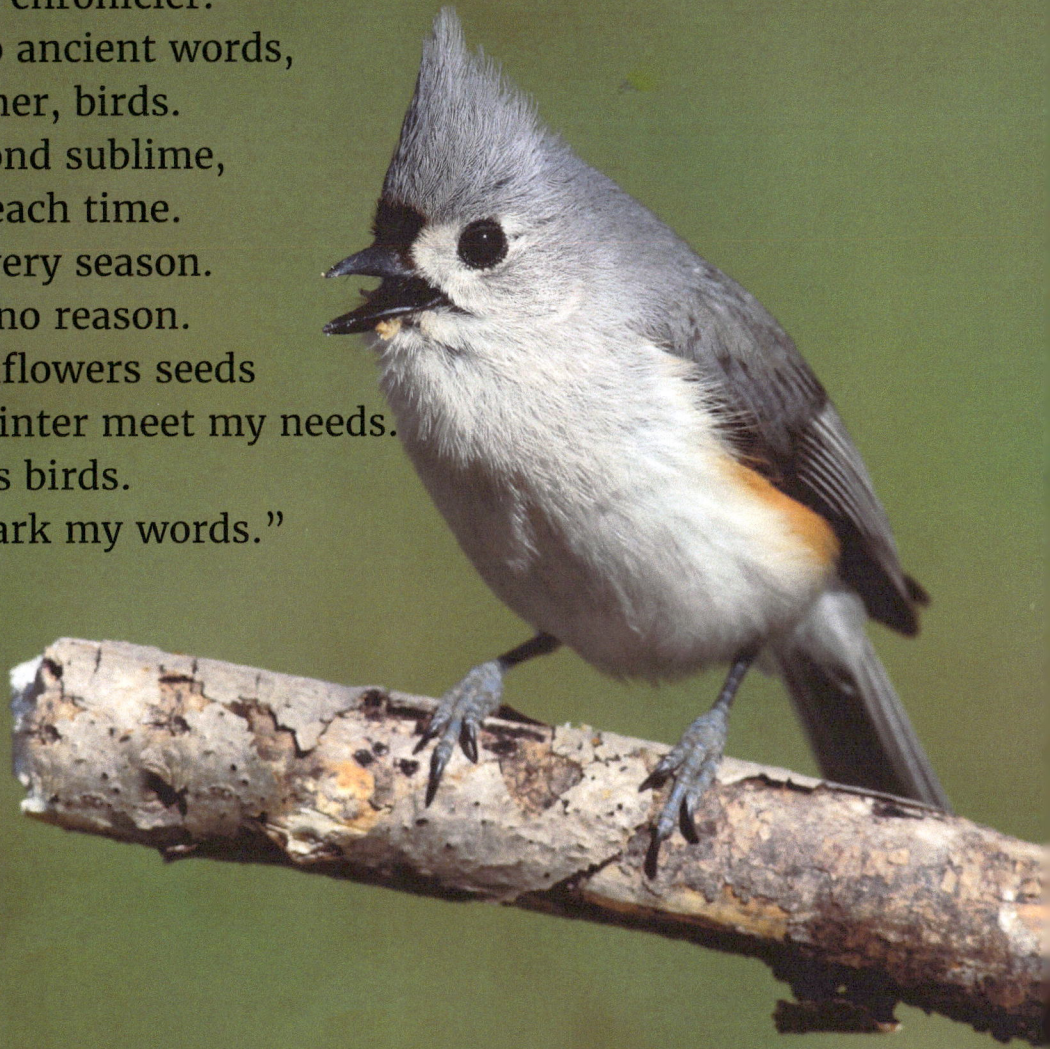

Tufted Titmouse

Orange as a color name was unknown in English until the 16th century, when oranges started to be imported into Britain from Spain. Birders can occasionally spot tipsy robins in the late winter and early spring, thanks to fermented berries they have eaten.

THE AMERICAN ROBIN

"An American Robin, I was fated
To be named for a bird who's not related.
England called him 'Robinred,'
Orange was not a color said.
We're not red, it's a mistake,
A habit that we cannot break.
My head with feathers black will be
In mating season, you will see.
I eat worms but berries are fine.
In the spring, they taste like wine.
You may think that this is funny:
Robin eggs from the Easter bunny.
You've heard this bird and you must agree,
A very special king I'll be."

Doves are fast flyers and average 30-40 mph, but when alarmed they can reach 60 mph.

THE MOURNING DOVE

"I know it may sound mournful coo,
It is my song to share with you.
I hope the beauty will show through,
The ladies really like it, too.
A song of peacefulness I sing,
Tranquility is what I bring.
When I am near, please fill your feeder,
A Mourning Dove is such an eater.
If you see my feathers fly,
Then I've escaped up to the sky.
My flight is straight and bullet fast,
Helps me escape a hunter's blast.
I have black spots found on each wing;
I qualify to be your king."

Barn Owls have exceptional hearing that allows them to capture prey in complete darkness. Also, their eyesight is twice as sensitive as is a human's.

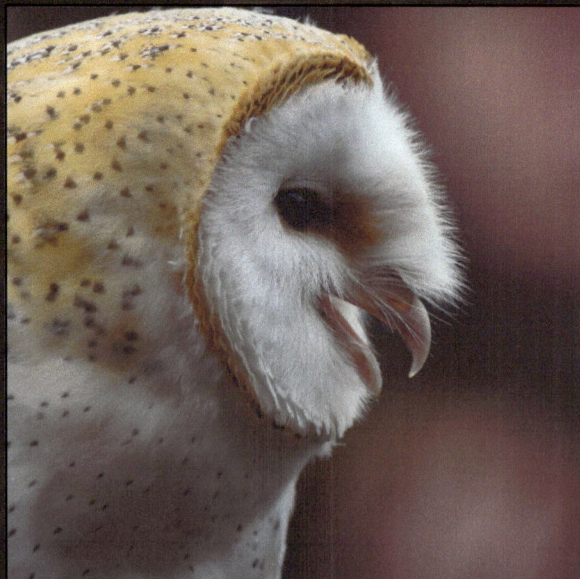

THE BARN OWL

"I'm here by day to meet you all,
Then I will nap until nightfall.
Barn Owls sleep in daytime hours,
Then are night owls with superpowers.
Cloaked hunter when completely dark,
I can see my moving mark.
I don't hoot, instead I screech,
This is my chosen form of speech.
I hiss at danger, dance in love.
Black stripes on my wings above.
I don't want to sound bombastic,
But there is no one as fantastic.
I'm your king, make no mistake,
There is no other choice to make.

Hummingbirds do not suck nectar through their long bills, instead they lick it with fringed, forked tongues.

Anna's Hummingbird

Fiery-Throated Hummingbird

Green Violet-Eared Hummingbird

White-Necked Jacobin

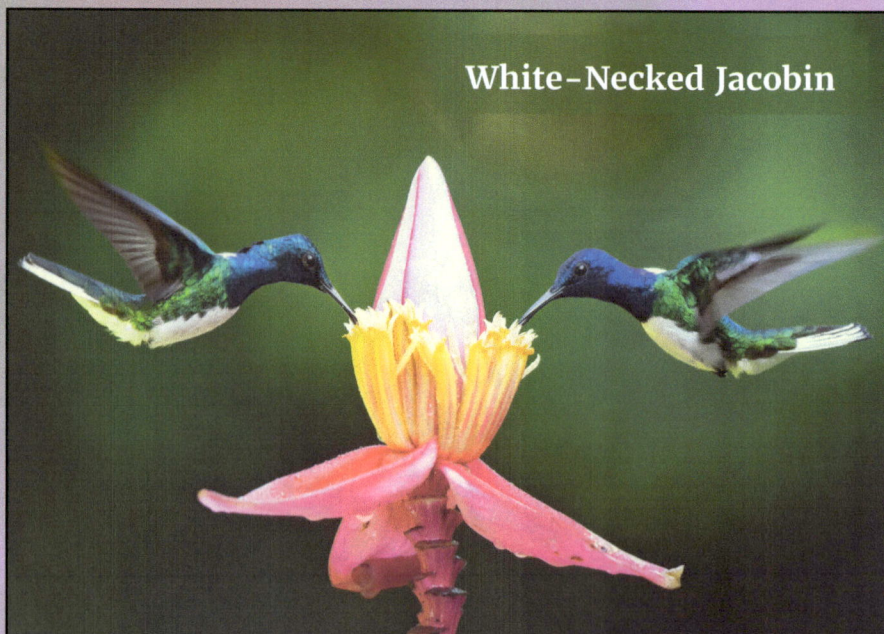

THE RUBY-THROATED HUMMINGBIRD

"Barely seen and barely heard,
I'm part stealth fighter and part bird.
Sixty miles per hour downhill,
Catch me if you see me still.
Frontwards, backwards, upside down,
I might be small bit like a clown.
This hummingbird's a happy guy,
You hear me hum whenever I fly.
Metallic green with white below,
My red gorget is such a show.
Nothing black, but king I'd be
Based only on velocity."

The Pewee prefers to sing after sunset and before the dawn, singing quite late in the evening, after most birds have fallen silent. Population declined by about 51% between 1966 and 2015.

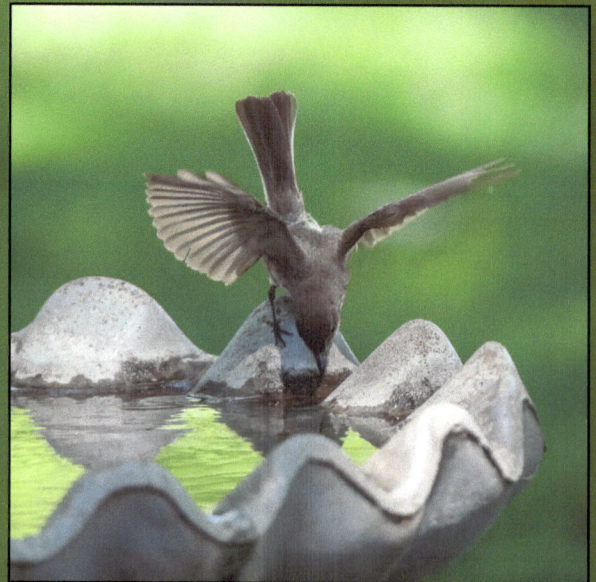

THE PEWEE

"I'm named after my 'pee-a-wee' call,
It's not 'peewee' and I'm not that small.
I'd rather sing when others gone,
After sunset, before the dawn.
Pewee groups are called dribbles or squirts,
Not certain why, just how it works.
Love my insects, caught mid-air,
Come flying near me if you dare.
Gray body, white throat, yellow belly, dark wings,
Bill top black, no feathery things.
I can't be king, I'm sure you guessed,
It seems I did not pass the test."

The red color of the male house finches' head and breast come from the pigments in the food that this bird is eating. Females prefer to mate with red males, because this means that the male can provide appropriate food for their chicks.

Chaffin's Finch

House Finch

White-winged Crossbill

Purple Finch

THE HOUSE FINCH

"Now I am hip," the House Finch said,
"I'm mostly brown with red on my head.
The girls prefer the reddest guys.
No black, so can't get kingly prize.
I love nectar, salt is fine.
My colors from on what I dine.
Darwin surely saw the most,
Fourteen on Galapagos.
I don't really understand
Why black makes you so brashly grand.
This is something I can't let go,
I should be the king, you know."

In French, *gros* means large. "Grosbeak" comes from the large size of his beak. Grosbeaks are known for singing on moonlit nights, sometimes all night, but never very loudly.

The Rose-breasted Grosbeak

Grosbeak said, "I'm ready now
To be your king, when you'll allow.
I have my splendid black and white,
And my red bib is dynamite.
My large beak is a Roman classic,
The ladies find it quite fantastic
I have a mellow warbling song,
I may sing all day and all night long.
When it's my turn with eggs in our nest,
Quietly I sing my best.
I am so far above the rest,
Since black and white and red are best."

"One for Sorrow" is a traditional children's nursery rhyme about Magpies. The most common version is a counting rhyme that goes to ten. According to an old superstition, the number of Magpies seen together tells if one will have bad or good luck.

THE MAGPIE

Called simply Pie in times gone past,
Maggie Pie has come to last.
"Bad luck, good luck, what do you see?
You can always count on me.
'One for sorrow, Two for joy,
Three for a girl, Four for a boy.'
One feather a sign of fearlessness,
I may be somewhat larcenous.
I hunt mostly in the spring,
Songbirds' eggs and young are my thing.
You see I'm big and black and white,
You should make me king outright."

Many of the Oystercatchers strike the shells to make a hole to get in. Oystercatchers can be right- or left-handed with their bill, striking to the left or to the right.

Parcel of American Oystercatchers

THE AMERICAN OYSTERCATCHER

The Oystercatcher from the coast
May have impressed them all the most.
He was, in fact, a beautiful creature.
His bill was his most striking feature.
His eyes hypnotic, bored through things,
Yellow centers, orange rings.
His head and chest were black so he
Could be their king quite definitely.
The others giggled when they heard
That he was first called sea pie bird.
"I am different, and consequently,
I will rule you differently."

In fact, warblers may be a mix of colors. Brilliant yellow color is most common.

Cerulean Warbler

Blackburnian Warble

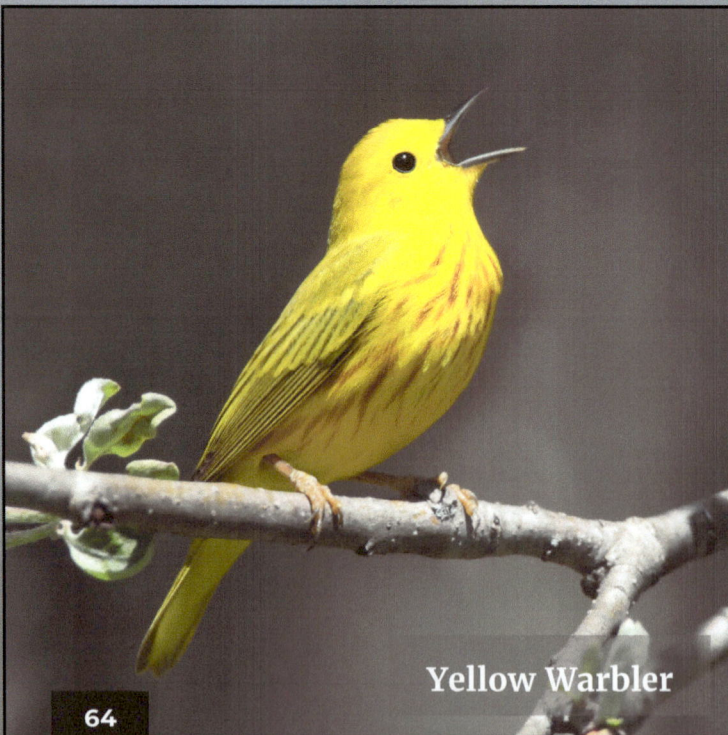

Yellow Warbler

Prothonotary Warbler

THE BLACK-AND-WHITE WARBLER

Warbler next came into sight,
One with stripes of black and white.
Trills and quavers, warblers' song,
Walking tree trunks all along.
"I eat insects; hear my words,
Birdseed is for other birds.
Maybe this just my reaction,
Fancy colors are a distraction.
Black and white are royal colors,
There is no need for any others.
It's an easy thing to see,
I am the Birdland king-to-be."

Acorn Woodpecker

Woodpeckers don't peck at night. They roost at night and are mostly quiet. Woodpeckers have special feathers that cover their nostrils to prevent dust and splinters of wood from getting in the way.

Ladder Back Woodpecker

THE DOWNY WOODPECKER

Who's that knocking on the door,
And the window and the floor?
If Woodpecker becomes the king,
There may be holes in everything!
"When I am king, I promise you,
Only black and white will do.
If on me a bit of red,
Doesn't count when on my head.
Other colors welcome here,
'Though they put you toward the rear.
There will be justice, wait and see,
Some more if you should look like me.
I am the best you will agree,
The black and white king I will be."

King Vulture

THE VULTURE

A Vulture stood by silently
And thought how little birds can be:
Too proud, too noisy, narrow-minded,
Arrogant, and simply blinded.
"You want to be elected king?
Reconsider what you bring.
It isn't how you look, you see,
Just take a careful look at me.
It's not your nest or how you fly
Or what you sing when you fly by.
It's in your heart and how you treat
The other birds that you might meet.
Selfish birds make me see red.
It's too bad they're not yet dead."

Vulture mostly dines on carrion,
The opposite of a vegetarian.
Birds may not know what's ahead,
They're not eaten until they're dead.

The Catbirds get their name from their call that resembles the 'meow' of a cat.

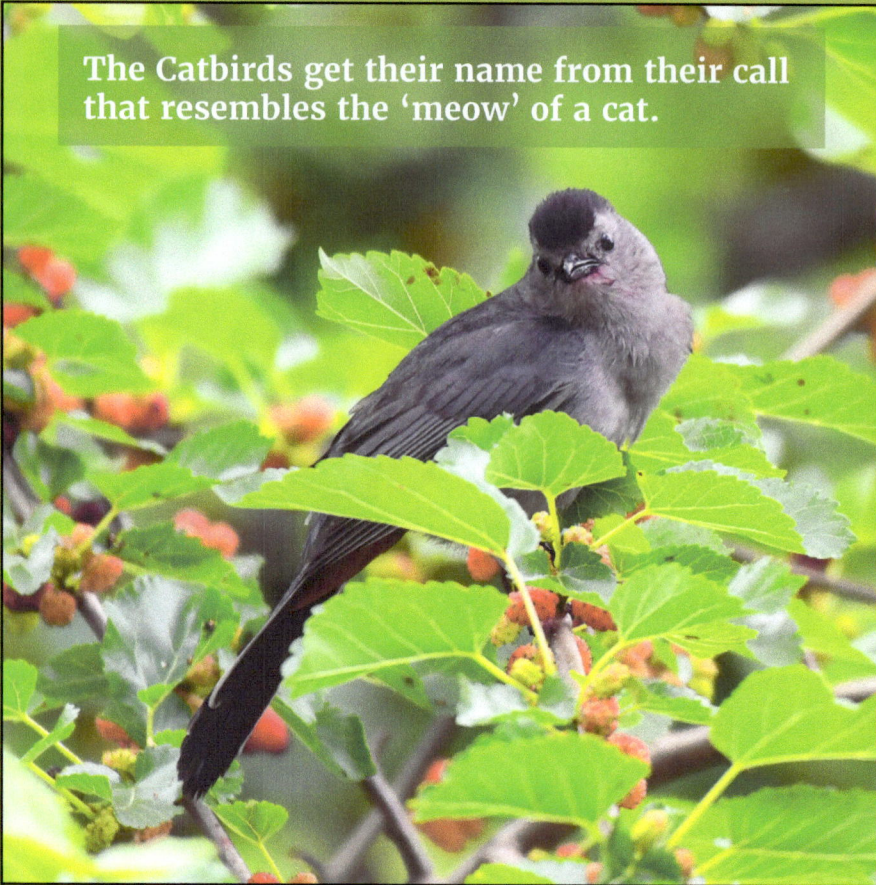

THE GRAY CATBIRD

"I've heard you tell why you are best,
But tell us how you help the rest.
There are different ways to sing
And different kinds of coloring.
You might prefer the one like you,
Yours not the only point of view.
When we are searching for our king,
Let me propose an important thing:
Whoever's king must know to do
Whatever's best for both me and you,
No matter the feathers on your wing
Or where you live or how you sing.
You may seem to lose advantage.
I'm sure that somehow you will manage."

The Catbird made this observation,
Yet still it met with consternation.
"I've had a chance for some reflection,
I now will run in this election.
And all the birds no matter colors
Should join the search with all the others."

As a symbol of immortality, rebirth and life after death. In Christianity, the resurrected Phoenix became a popular symbol for how Jesus Christ has risen from the grave.

THE PHOENIX

The birds could not believe their eyes
When there appeared to their surprise
The one described in history,
Exceptional its destiny,
Symbol of self-sacrifice,
Rebirth comes yet at a price.
Phoenix dies on funeral pyre
As the flames go high and higher.
New Phoenix would from ash arise
Now came to them, what to apprise?
"Seeing what looks like the end
Is simply chance for fresh begin.
Overlook what might divide,
Peace and goodness be your guide.
Kindness and sincerity
Should not be a rarity."

THE MAGPIE REPLIES

The magpie took the microphone.
"Black and white is all I've known.
When you look with brighter light,
The little catbird may be right
That feather colors aren't the thing
That count toward making a good king.
So we start with new attitude
That will take some fortitude,
But I know we have the aptitude
And import of some magnitude.
Acceptance really is the key,
It's simply how things best should be."

Catbird, vulture smile they would
If any of the kingdom could.

Unlike mammals, birds lack facial muscles
attached to their skull. Therefore, they
cannot show a common expression such as a
frown or a smile.

The Catbird was elected king.
The Vulture stationed by his wing
Was there to help with any ol' thing.

www.ingramcontent.com/pod-product-compliance
Lightning Source LLC
Chambersburg PA
CBHW061140030426

42335CB00002B/53